Anand Karaj - The Sikhing View
(The good, the bad and the ugly)

AUTHOR
UNCLE DYA SINGH

Published by Consultsingh
PO Box 77, Doveton, 3177, Australia

First Published August 2025

www.CulturalEducation.com.au

Author: Uncle Dya Singh
Illustrator: Neil Cavagan
Editors
Jamel Kaur Singh
Johanna Marie Ferrer

ISBN 978-0-9756100-9-1

Produced by Consultsingh Pty. Ltd.

I am grateful for the encouragement and support by

Dr. Devinder Singh Grewal and Mrs. Surinder Kaur Grewal

of the renowned GREWAL FAMILY of Port Augusta, South Australia

celebrating the Anand Karaj of their beloved maternal grandson

Lucas, to Selina on 22nd March 2025

and in loving memory of Lucas' beloved late mother

Rupinder who passed away on 11th July 2016.

28 years before on the same date as the Anand Karaj of Selina and Lucas, I had the honour of conducting the Anand Karaj of Rupinder to David Hazel, the parents of Lucas. Her untimely passing away in 2016 was a sad loss.

Dya Singh

circa 1960s L-R: Kaka Dya Singh s/o Giani Harchand Singh on the harmonium, Giani Harchand Singh Ji and Moti Ram Ji on the tabla performing an Anand Karaj at old Shapan Gurdwara, Chan Sow Lin Road, Sungei Besi, Kuala Lumpur.

A Note from the Author

After almost 7 decades of involvement with the Sikh sacred marriage ceremony called 'Anand Karaj', firstly as a member of the holy congregation (sangat), spectator when it turns into a spectacle, assisting my venerable father Giani Harchand Singh Ji of 'Bassian' in the ceremony, and also personally conducting for almost half a century, I have seen the good, the bad and the ugly.

I have seen some very blissful spiritually uplifting ceremonies when one can sense that it augurs well for the couple into their future. I have seen ignorance of the spiritual import of the ceremony. I have seen callous behaviour and irreverence, wardrobe malfunctions and comical antics of couples, chiefly grooms, mainly due to ignorance or lack of preparedness or just getting carried away with the pomp and ceremony.

Some of the ceremonies that I have witnessed especially over the last 3 decades or so, appear to have become public spectacles, of entertainment value and enactments for filming! In some cases, the mere dressing of the couple can be quite comical!

I want couples who intend to go through the ceremony to know that they do not, firstly, have to be trussed up like peacocks and be in discomfort because of their costumes just because their parents went through that experience or they assume that that is the norm, or forgetting that unlike 'western' weddings, they have to be able to bow with reverence, 'metha-tek' (touch their forehead on the ground before Guru Ji – Sri Guru Granth Sahib Ji), sit down cross-legged and stand up, unassisted.

We need to differentiate presumed cultural demands and traditions from the pristine essence of the spiritual import of this sacred ceremony.

The couple need to present themselves before Guru Ji in total humility for His Blessings, dressed in comfortable yet elegant clothing. For couples outside India, I still do not understand why couples and their parents have to go back to India just to get decked up for the Anand Karaj!

The bride should be able to walk behind her husband without holding up her cumbersome and heavy 'lehnga', which has been tied halfway up her waist because it is too long, with one hand, while holding the marital scarf (pela) with the other!

I have seen grooms giving the thumbs up or waving to their friends in the sangat as they go through the 'lavan'!

There are ways and means of injecting joy into the ceremony without bloopers, comedic antics by the couple and avoidable wardrobe malfunctions for the bemusement of the sangat.

So, over 70 odd years I have witnessed that the ceremony has, generally, evolved into a noisy, colourful, celebratory ritual with scant spiritual substance, or even sidelined as a secondary part of a 'wedding celebration'.

This book is to assist couples and parents of couples, even the congregation (sangat) and those conducting, as a guide and reflection upon the spiritual import of the ceremony, to assist the couple towards a life-long and fulfilling married life, life as householders the Sikhi way.

True to my nature it is a fun book to read with some anecdotes of the follies I have witnessed, but also the spiritual nourishment it can provide if attention is put towards it.

Today, in general, rather than being the most important, the ceremony is inadvertently relegated to 2nd position behind the 'Reception' and sometimes 3rd after even the *Milni* (formal 'meeting' of the two families), or a recent development called 'sangeet night'.

Table of Contents

INTRODUCTION

Anand Karaj (Sikh sacred marriage ceremony) – normally passed off as the 'Ceremony of Bliss', is the **Ceremony of Equipoise**, towards a marital life of spiritual/material balance - *Grahast Marag,* the life of a householder.

Anand is generally understood as being in bliss. Bliss has an expiry date. Everyday bliss is tied to fleeting experiences. A baby with a full stomach, with a clean and dry nappy and not in pain is in bliss. Anand as in Anand Karaj is about a state of serene acceptance – being at peace with oneself, that where there is joy there is sorrow; where there is comfort and wellbeing there is also pain and dis-ease and finally where there is life there is death too.

Anand anand sabh ko kehai, anand Guru te janeya … (Anand Sahib) {Bliss, bliss, everyone talks of bliss, but bliss is only known through the Guru}.

Central to a deeper understanding of *anand* is the 40 stanza Gurbani (scripture) called Anand Sahib. It is the profound joy which comes with spiritual wisdom through meditation, introspection and internal calm – a lifelong journey of gradually falling in love with the Divine with a soulmate by your side. Six of the 40 stanzas which are sung after the ceremony are interpreted in brief further forward.

Many other religious/faith groups including Muslims and Catholics have **pre-marriage courses**. In Malaysia I recollect Islamic agencies which carry out such courses called 'Kursus Perkahwinan'.

> ...the spiritual aspects (*of Anand Karaj*) are the glue that holds marital life together... for life. So, even within the mundane we seek the spiritual.

The 'Sikhiya' (Marriage Sermon) offered at the ceremony or even any attempts to put information down in writing normally stresses the religious or spiritual aspects of this ceremony when marriage is about grappling with the mundane – the realities. Without doubt the spiritual aspects are the glue that holds marital life together, to battle the mundane, for life. So, even within the mundane we seek the spiritual.

{What I mean by **spirituality** *is the search for the Truth – the meaning, purpose and pursuit of the ultimate 'divine' reality which is beyond the limitations of time, and human intellect, but can be felt. By* **mundane** *I mean everyday living as a human being.*

To ensure that we are not wholly talking about God in the Abrahamic sense, we shall use terms like the Divine, Creator or the Sikh terms like Waheguru – Wonderous Teacher (the WOW factor), and Akal Purakh – the Eternal Male (implying that all of Creation is of the feminine gender).} The 'Sikh' God is discussed in brief further along.

Spiritual progress as 'one soul in two bodies' *(Aik jyot doay moorthi…)* is the primordial thrust associated with Anand Karaj.

Old Sikh texts like *Prem Sumarag*, various 'HukmNamas' and even the Sikh *Reht Maryadha* (Code of Conduct) stress on the religious/spiritual aspects of a Sikh marriage. And being from a strong patriarchal background like most faith and religious groups, these texts also, unwittingly, place greater stress on the duties and subservience of the 'wife' rather than a balanced approach between both partners in a marriage as Sikh philosophy intends. So, the only source which can be relied upon for true spiritual guidance is the constant pillar, 'guru' – Sri Guru Granth Sahib.

This is an attempt to offer a more balanced view – the need of life today and into the future – specifically, advice on the mundane besides the spiritual, and the Sikh view on gender equality.

The first 'lav' (1st of 4 hymns about Anand Karaj) starts – *Har Pehledi laav parvirti karam dirdahea Balram Jio… .(SGGSp773)* (explained in full in Part3).

The cue comes from the word *'parvirti',* which means engrossed in the phenomenon of human life, and here it implies grappling with the mundane reality of living – materialism, family and so on (*maya*).

Parvirth nirvirth hattha dovai vich dharam phirai raibarea…SGGSp1280. Attachment and detachment, involvement in the phenomenon of human life, and transcending it, are the two sides of this life, of which 'dharma' (true spiritual life duty) is the guide.

This is also an attempt to reflect humankind becoming a global village – social/spiritual evolution, the overlapping of cultures, changes in attitudes, 'mixed' marriages, shifting roles of the male and female, and the involvement of older traditions giving rise to new ones.

The basics and pillars of Sikhism and Guru Ji, the Sri Guru Granth Sahib Ji do not change but otherwise 'change' is the only constant in this human life.

```
The basics and pillars of Sikhism and Guru Ji,
  the Sri Guru Granth Sahib do not change but
otherwise 'change' is the only constant in this
                 human life.
```

I have always communicated with couples who request me to conduct their Anand Karaj with broadly four main emails sent to them and their parents as a pre-Anand Karaj 'course'. I am retaining those four 'sections' in this book.

The 4 sections are:

a. Basic views and criteria and some pertinent pre-marriage questions for today's generation of young Sikh professionals.
b. Working a run-sheet for the ceremony and the pitfalls and Sikh-centric practices to be aware of.
c. The spiritual thrust and the Lavan (**Sikhiya**) and a brief comment on the Sikh God.
d. *Betisulakhani* – Mundane (feminine) attributes for marital bliss and pitfalls based on gurmuth (basic Sikh philosophy).

There is a 5th Sundry section for further commentary on my observations on current state of the ceremony which will be amusing to some, concerning to the pious and perhaps offensive to the more traditional (fundamentalists). But this is the status quo, including my views on 'destination' weddings (I have conducted quite a number) which are currently frowned upon by Akaal Takhat edict. (Akaal Takhat is the seat of the Guru Panth, based within the precinct of Darbar Sahib (the Golden Temple) in Amritsar, Punjab, India.)

The days when some luminary like a *brahmgiani* (Sikh savant) or a scholar used to come to the podium just before the ceremony and deliver a meaningful sermon on Anand Karaj which was virtually a discourse not only in Sikhi living but on Sikhism itself, are long gone.

Today, the 'Sikhiya' is virtually non-existent, hence the need for some information or a course along these lines. Anyway, 'Sikhiya' from the pulpit is never consistent. It depends on the thoughts, reflections, experiences or hastily compiled notes of the deliverer. There is plenty of information for the layman on the Anand Karaj on google now.

This is an attempt to reflect changing life patterns, and the growing proportion of mixed marriages, or at least facilitating further discussion. This merely opens the door to further self-research, reflection, introspection, awareness and curiosity leading to an individual's spiritual advancement – or in this case, as a couple, the Sikhi way. Most importantly we need to be aware that there is more to the Anand Karaj than just the ritualistic and entertainment thrust.

It is also fashionable presently to write a one-page synopsis of what an Anand Karaj is, as an insert into the marriage invitation card or handed out to guests as they arrive. Perhaps there is enough information here to write up that synopsis rather than a randomly selected translation of the 4 'lavan' which at best is normally confusing and seldom read by anyone!

1

REFLECTIONS & CRITERIA & SOME PERTINENT PRE-ANAND KARAJ QUESTIONS

The 4 circumambulations (slow walk clockwise around the Sikh 'guru', Sri Guru Granth Sahib by the couple) to the strains of the *Gurbani* (the 'word' or scripture, from the Guru) of the 4 *'lavan'* (the 4 scriptural passages about Sikh marital life) firstly signifies the couple stepping into marital bliss but then reminding them of moving from worldly love for each other as two human beings into a strong loving bond, as one spirit, with the Divine.

> The Anand Karaj … signifies the couple stepping into marital bliss but then reminding them of moving from worldly love for each other as two human beings into a strong loving bond, as one spirit, with the Divine.

Though the spiritual journey is as an individual, the Anand Karaj prepares one to continue the human part of that journey with a partner with the Sri Guru Granth Sahib Ji as being symbolic of the Creator and as the Guru, the Divine Teacher. That signifies that the couple will look to the Guru Granth Sahib as their 'Guru', for the duration of their lives and the upbringing of their offsprings. These spiritual undertones make the Anand Karaj unique compared to any other marriage ceremony.

Over my lifetime I have seen many changes in Anand Karaj. *(By the way I was born and spent my formative years in Malaysia and living in gurdwaras as I am the son of a Sikh gurmuth teacher, kirtenia, Granthi Sahib and a savant.)*

Up to the late 1950's a couple intending to go through the Anand Karaj were expected to have undergone the **Amrit Sanchar** and become members of the **Khalsa Fraternity** (the fraternity of the Pure, or God's own). Roughly between 1960-70 in my experience, couples were questioned before the ceremony as to whether they had undergone *Amrit Sanchar* and if not to agree to go through the Amrit Sanchar as soon as the next ceremony was availed to them. Slowly over the preceding decades that requirement became optional, and today the question does not even arise.

I do, however, believe that if, as a couple, you have no intention of living as Sikhs and bringing up the offsprings with Sikhi knowledge, then the *Anand Karaj* appears to be superfluous except for its ritualistic, colourful, entertaining and celebratory attraction.

I have witnessed some rather amusing mishaps in recent times during the ceremony because in many cases the couple has no knowledge of what the ceremony is about nor any proper rehearsal, let alone any information nor instruction. Couples who have barely seen the inside of a gurdwara or what protocol is required before the Guru Granth Sahib are clearly disadvantaged and their antics to being instructed in every step adds to the bemusement of those witnessing the ceremony.

Some Embarrassing Examples

a. The groom who has a ready-made turban placed on his head just for the ceremony seeing it drop off his head as he bows (*metha tek*) to Guru Ji.

b. Groom's 'pajama' splits as he bends down to 'metha-tek' as it is brand new and too tight!

c. The groom starts walking in the wrong direction before being corrected, sometimes pulled back by the bride!

d. The bride is so heavily veiled and further weighed down with thick clothing, jewellery, arms filled with shining bangles to the elbows, and dried coconut kernels tied to her wrists, that she needs to be 'led' (as she is unable to see in front of her and straining under the weight of her costume and jewellery), assisted to bow (*metha-tek*) and helped to sit down cross-legged and get up when needed like a helpless invalid!

e. The bride comes in with a long 'train' (as they do in western white weddings) leading to pandemonium when it comes to doing the circumambulations around the Guru Ji.

f. The bride insists on a coterie of 'maids-of-honour' all dressed in exactly the same dresses, aping western culture and the poor young ladies not knowing what to do with themselves as the Anand Karaj is taking place.

g. Inappropriate dressing. What could pass off at any other 'wedding' could be considered immodest at an Anand Karaj.
    We arrive in the court of Guru Ji in utter humility craving for His Blessings. To be dressed gaudily, overdressed, or scantily clothed is distasteful. I have seen it all. In fact, simple, modest dressing with ease of movement and sitting down cross-legged should be considered.

h. **Camera-crew** is there to 'discreetly' record the memorable, moving landmark ceremony in the life of the couple. They are not there to use the ceremony as a

prop to produce a movie! Of prime importance is the sanctity of the ceremony. (I have seen camera crew virtually 'directing' the ceremony, and they are not normally appropriately dressed either.)

How many issues can you pick with this scene?

Protocol expected in the 'darbar' of Guru Granth Sahib Ji should be observed – heads covered, no veils on faces, respectful 'Sunday best' dressing by all, (including sangat and camera crew) to cater for the ability to sit down cross-legged, footwear to be removed outside, and respectful silence in Darbar Sahib. No alcohol, drugs or tobacco items are allowed and hopefully no hangovers from a 'big' night before (stag or hen parties or now, the 'sangeet night').

Wardrobe Malfunctions

His face says it all!

(Even though a rehearsal is done, the couple should also go through the motions of 'metha'tek', sit down cross-legged and get up from the cross-legged position after wearing their costumes for the ceremony with especial attention to below)

a. Groom: Does the turban, if tied for the occasion only, or a ready-made one placed on his head, stay on his head even when he is bowing?

b. Is the costume, especially *pajama* or trousers loose enough not to split when the groom bends down to 'metha-tek?

c. Bride: Does the head-covering stay firm on the hairline? Are pins needed to hold it in position? (The face must be visible, and the head covering should not leave any part of the head uncovered.)

d. Are the overall dress and ornaments just too heavy and cumbersome? Can any changes be made to lighten the burden?

e. If wearing bangles, are they of the right size?

f. Anklets can be a nuisance. They catch the dress bottom and cause entanglements.

g. Early morning hair-do's. I have known of up to 2 hours seen delay on the Anand Karaj day because of problems with doing up the hair for the bride for the big occasion.

Some Positive Examples

1. An Anand Karaj which took place at 7am after all involved sat down to listen to Asa Dhi Var (a morning musical prayer) from 5am. It was a very simple, spiritually charged solemn ceremony. The couple presented themselves in simple off-white clothing. Most moving. One could feel the transformation of a couple in love into a divine union with the Guru.
2. Couple arrived together, dressed in simple yet elegant off-white *kudta-pajama* (simple Punjabi clothes) bowing humbly before Guru Ji and sitting down immediately for their *Anand Karaj*.
3. In an *Anand Karaj* held in a hall, the couple performed the *smapti* (retirement ceremony) of Guru Ji immediately after the ceremony. Then the groom reverently took Guru Ji on his head with his bride doing *chaur-sewa* (flowing the flywhisk over Guru Ji), as Guru Ji was the first to leave the hall with full pomp and ceremony.
4. In all the 'destination' *Anand Karaj* I have conducted, the Guru Ji is the last to arrive and the first to leave. Full respect is always accorded to Guru Ji, as would be expected of a dignitary.

Ideally the most touching ceremony and one which will augur well for the lifelong wedded bliss of the couple is that where the couple take an interest in finding out what the ceremony is about, accepting it for its sacred and spiritual import, and coming before Guru Ji in a humble and meditative frame of mind craving for Guru Ji's Grace and a divine union with Him.

```
One could feel the transformation of a couple in
                love into a divine
              union with the Guru.
```

Criteria

The Sikh Rehat Maryadha (Code of Conduct) stipulates that only a Sikh man and a Sikh woman can be married through the *Anand Karaj*. Though this is now not adhered to, I believe that a couple intending to marry should only consider the *Anand Karaj* if they expect to keep a lifelong association with Sikh spirituality (through *'shabad khoj'*) and expect to bring up their offsprings in the *Sikhi* way of life. {Shabad khoj – personal research and introspection into Gurbani and *sadh-sangat* – company of Sikh holy congregation.}

Going through an Anand Karaj perhaps just to appease the wishes of one partner or parents and relatives is undermining the deep sacred thrust of the one ceremony. An alternative perhaps, is a registry marriage followed by a service (Jord Mela) before Guru Ji, based on the Anand Karaj.

So, especially in the case of a 'mixed' marriage (where one partner is not of the Sikh faith) this question should be seriously addressed. But after such reflection if a couple still wishes to go through the Anand Karaj, then they should. It is their right and of course, if the gurudwara management accepts. One gurdwara council in a state in India, in its infinite wisdom has recently banned mixed marriages, especially inter-faith marriages.

It has also become common practice where a 'mixed' couple is concerned, to have two ceremonies – one each in the two faith or religious groups the couple belongs to. Two ceremonies presumably being better than one, more celebrations, or to please both sets of parents and relatives. But this further appears to defeat the purpose of truly understanding the deep sacred import of a sacred ceremony, certainly in the case of the Anand Karaj as I understand it. Surely vows before God Almighty should only be taken once. An additional 'registration' mainly for legal purposes is understandable.

Some Pertinent Pre-Anand Karaj Questions

(Based on my observations on why marriages break up. They are to some extent rhetorical.)

To counter the blindness of 'falling in love' as the main ingredient for marriage, couples should ask each other some pertinent questions to be able to rationally assess whether they are compatible as marriage partners.

a. Are both of you on the same page as to the number of offsprings you have in mind or none, or, as Sikhi advocates, leave it to the blessings (Hukm) of Waheguru? *(There are individuals that do not wish to have any children for a variety of reasons or prefer to adopt. Also ask each other, what happens if we do not conceive, or can't conceive?)*

b. Where do you intend to stay? Do you have a home ready for you to move in? What are your long-term intentions about a home?

c. Are you going to be responsible for any of your parents in their old age? Traditionally that was taken for granted. Expectations of the wife becoming a part of the groom's parental household and forsaking her own parents, rarely applies now and should not. Has this issue been discussed? For most Sikh couples the question does not even arise. It is understood and expected that the couple will be fully responsible for their parents till they pass on. But, the reality of today's western thought, that parents will end up in the old folks' homes, must be addressed. And parents should know that well in advance.

d. Are your parents dictating everything for the ceremony or should you, as a couple be directly involved in arrangements as it is 'your' ceremony and your future? Are your parents going to run your lives into the future as well or are they there to be of assistance, support and guidance?

e. Do you need a pre-marital contract? Legal documents? (These days this is done to avoid complications on a breakup and perhaps for tax reasons.)

f. In a 'mixed' marriage situation, there are muted expectations within certain religions that the partner must convert for marriage. Such clarifications need to be made before marriage. What baptism (if any) are your off spring going to undertake, what last rights will be performed? How / who will name your children?

g. Again, in a mixed couple scenario – what faith group do you wish to instruct and bring up your offsprings – mum's, or dad's? The question is a serious one as children do need some form of moral/spiritual upbringing. There is a saying – it takes a village to bring up a child. The 'community' is the village in modern times. What kind of moral, ethical and social etiquette education will they provide their offsprings? The answer 'we will let them decide when they are old enough' is a lame one. Children need some form of spiritual guidance from birth.

Offsprings will certainly decide when they are old enough but meanwhile what manner of instructions and upbringing on morality, societal conforms, etiquette, ethics and spirituality are you going to organise for them? What is the input into the child's memory bank? *(Most religious or faith groups I know of do have elements of such basic upbringing.)* This will determine a child's temperament and nature into adulthood.

Formal western schooling does not deal with that or at best it is inadequate.

This is also a valid question for couples born within the Sikh faith. You will have to be actively involved in their spiritual upbringing and perhaps even might have to self-educate further to be able to teach them. Just taking them to gurdwara occasionally is inadequate.

(A trivial note on upbringing of children: Over my lifetime I have noticed changes in behaviour of the younger generations. When we were young, for example, we were taught to make guests

feel welcome and play host in the absence of the parents or other elders. These days children barely talk to guests. Most are engrossed with their I-phones or I-pads! Social etiquette, ethics, spiritual awareness, moral standards and mother tongue are the educational responsibilities of parents and grandparents in the first instance.)

The 4th monkey – hears, speaks and sees no one.

2

A TENTATIVE 'RUN SHEET' FOR
THE ANAND KARAJ

It is important to work a 'run sheet' for the ceremony to get all parties on the same page. Sometimes an elder, for example, steps forward during the ceremony to insist that a certain procedure must be carried out! Except to add to the amusement of the sangat as hasty changes are made, it is but an unnecessary intrusion.

Example 1: After the first circumambulation a couple decided in the spur of the moment that they will stand, in between the circumambulations. An elder quickly got up and insisted that they sit. There was a commotion holding up the ceremony before the elder's insistence was accepted and the couple reluctantly sat down. (The older generations prefer the couple to *metha-tek* and sit down but some amongst the current generations just wish to stand.) (*Metha-tek: Bowing deeply and touching the forehead to the ground before Guru Ji before sitting down or standing up*).

Example 2: The grandmother of the groom insisted 'just' before the ceremony that a full Asa-Dhi-Var (morning musical prayer which normally takes about one and a half hour) must be sung or the ceremony would be incomplete. So her wish had to be carried out. The Anand Karaj was delayed by over an hour to the frustration of all.

Some Important Pointers

Neither the bride nor groom should have their faces covered (no veils of any kind) when presenting themselves before the Guru. (The 'sehra' covering the face of the groom which some insist upon, must be removed before entering the Darbar Sahib.)

There should be no bridesmaids, flower girls, nor groomsmen. The bride could have some close female friend/s or relative/s to attend to her at the ceremony. The groom has a 'servala' (best man) to be by his side for cultural purposes, but not during the ceremony.

It is preferable that the couple walk the 4 circumambulations on their own steam. However, some close relatives of the bride may stand towards the back of Guru Ji to see the couple through. Traditionally the maternal uncles and cousins of the bride are present, for support.

No confetti or flower petals should be thrown on the couple within the vicinity of Guru Ji. It is disrespectful to Guru Ji. However, such can be done as couple leave the Darbar Sahib.

Sikhism does not subscribe to any superstition that firstly the ceremony must be concluded before Noon. Nor do Sikhs subscribe to the notion that the ceremony can only take place in the morning, or even on a particular (auspicious) day. I have conducted an Anand Karaj at 4pm (after a cup of afternoon tea with some finger food) leading into the 'Reception'.

Tentative 'Runsheet' of the Ceremony with Some Further Pertinent Notes

Milni – the formal 'meet and greet' of the groom's party (braat, junj) by the bride's family normally with some gifts. *{This is tradition. The two 'families' would in most cases in the past be meeting for the first time – the bride's family plays host to the groom's family. Today it is optional. It can be made as elaborate as you like or simplified. A simple 'Hello, Welcome' and an affectionate hug can turn into an elaborate ceremony involving gifts or even gold ornaments given. Groom arrives on a white horse or in the spirit of one-upmanship, on an elephant! From personal experience, it cuts away into the time needed for the actual ceremony.*

Perhaps a tradition which needs to be reconsidered? It has its celebratory attraction. There is little spiritual significance in it except the Ardaas for harmony within the families coming together.}

Baraat Breakfast – normally the bride's party hosts the groom's party.

Divan – Kirtan (hymn singing) commences as sangat (congregation) file into the Darbar Sahib in the presence of Guru Granth Sahib Ji.

Arrival of couple – traditionally groom arrives before the bride but there are couples who wish to arrive together before Guru Ji.

Ongoing Simran, kirtan – (Main hymn: Keeta Lodiyay kam… invoking Guru Ji's Blessings to see the ceremony through as soon as the couple enters Guru Ji's presence). Hymn interpretation - See **Note 1**.

Welcoming Address by Celebrant/MC/Granthi Sahib.

Initial Ardaas (Standing Liturgy) – the couple and their parents stand as the Granthi Sahib does an Ardaas (standing Liturgy) mainly requesting Guru Ji's consent to proceed with the ceremony. The congregation (sangat) sits in silent meditation. (The Granthi Sahib can be male or female and is responsible for the readings from Guru Ji and the Ardaas.)

Hukm Nama – random passage read from Guru Ji and should be interpreted/translated. This is the 'blessing/advice' from Guru Ji. (I always request that a note is made of the HukmNama so that the couple can print it out with an interpretation and frame it, to remind them of their big day and the advice Guru Ji gave them.)

Sikhiya – the celebrant/MC delivers a short sermon on Anand Karaj especially the duties and responsibilities of the couple in married life. (This could be part of the 'Welcoming address'.)

Pela **Ceremony** – Giving away of the bride (Hymn – *Pelay thainday laagi* … 'we attach ourselves to You, O Lord, to follow the Guru's way…'). Hymn Intepretation – See **Note 2**.

The *'Lavan'*. See Interpretation of the 4 hymns – **Note 3**. *{There should be at least half an hour set aside just for this main part of the ceremony. A decision needs to be made beforehand whether the couple is* *going to remain standing when the 'lavan' are being read or whether they will 'metha tek' and sit down. Traditional preference is that the couple does 'metha-tek' and sit down in between the circumambulations in deep respect of the Gurbani being recited.}* (*Metha-tek*: Bowing deeply and touching the forehead to the ground before Guru Ji before sitting down or standing up.)

Hymn/s – *Veah hoa mere Babula…* (My marriage has taken place…) – **Note 4.** (*Other hymns may be sung. Sometimes the couple does some kirtan.)*

Concluding Kirtan, and address by a representative from the bride's party or a special guest – traditionally someone would write a poem about the couple, their parents and relatives called a *'sehra'* to be read after the *'lavan'*.

Anand Sahib (1st 5 stanzas & 40th stanza normally sung). See interpretation – **Note 5.**

Ardaas – Standing Liturgy for entire congregation thanking Guru Ji for the successful completion of the ceremony and blessings for the couple.

Hukm Nama (earlier HukmNama may be repeated)

Pershaadh (Sacred pudding) – first for couple who depart before the sangat leaves, unless it has been pre-arranged that Guru Ji leaves first, perhaps with the bride and groom part of that procession escorting Guru Ji out. This ensures that the sanctity of the Darbar Sahib is maintained at all times. Photography with relatives and congratulatory gestures etc. should be done outside of the Darbar Sahib.

Pertinent note to photography crew: Please be as unobtrusive and inconspicuous as possible. Station yourselves at vantage points. Movement by crew should be minimal. Do not follow the couple around the Guru Ji. You should not get in the line of sight of the sangat nor of the kirtan jatha from Guru Ji.

It is important that a run-sheet for the ceremony is discussed between the couple, parents, even grandparents, photographers and those conducting the ceremony and firmed up. A brief rehearsal too, should be carried out before the ceremony.

Note 1: Hymn – *Keeta Lodiyay kam so Har pai Aakhiyai…*

Before undertaking any project or such a ceremony, seek the Grace/permission of The Almighty. He will resolve your affairs. The True Guru gives His assurance of Truth. In the society of the saintly, you will taste the ambrosial nectar. The Merciful Lord erases all doubts and fears and protects His devotee. O Nanak, sing His glorious praises, He reveals Himself!

Note 2: Hymn– *Pelay thanday laagi …*

Praise and slander I banish from my mind. I take the marital sash (as my consent to be in union with you) and abandon all other worldly affairs. All other relationships I now deem illusory, time-bound, and I cling to Thee, my Lord. (A spiritual acceptance of the Almighty overseeing all affairs.)

Note 3: The 4 *'lavan'*.

O Creator, as we step forth into the **<u>first circumambulation</u>** we resolve to step onto the path of a householder with earthly marital duties. To carry out our earthly marital duties accepting your Word as our Guru, with Your Naam in our hearts and lips. We shall act righteously contemplating and meditating on Your Naam. All our sins and wrongs will be dispelled. Serene bliss is ours and we taste the sweet nectar of Your Naam. Nanak says – the union has begun.

In the **<u>second circumambulation</u>** we meet the True Guru, the Primordial Being – Waheguru. Realising Him ego is tamed, and we perceive Him everywhere. Nanak says, in the second circumambulation I feel Him everywhere.

In the **<u>third circumambulation</u>** the joy of detachment fills the mind. My company is with the faithful and with them I rejoice in His Naam. In the third circumambulation we are united with Him

In the **<u>fourth and final round</u>** our body and mind experience the Divine. We taste His sweetness day and night, all desires are fulfilled, the union is complete. In the fourth circumambulation we wed the Husband Lord.

Note 4: *Veah hoa mere Babula…* SGGSp78/9: My marriage has taken place, O my Beloved Lord. I aspire to be a Gurmukh (devotee). I have found my Lord. Darkness of ignorance is lifted. The Guru has revealed the light of spiritual wisdom. It shines bright. I have attained the priceless jewel of the Divine. My ego is dispelled, my pain is overcome. My 'I' identity, my ego self has been eradicated. The formless One is now my undying Form. He is imperishable and shall never leave me. My marriage is complete, and I am a true devotee.

Note 5: First 5 and the last (40th) stanzas of the Anand Sahib. (Only a synopsis of each stanza is given.)

1. Joy has welled up within. I have attained my True Guru. Celestial beings sing the Guru's words, and the music of bliss resounds within. I have found equipoise.
2. My soul, ever abide with Him. All suffering will be forgotten. He will arrange all your affairs. Abide with Him.
3. True Lord, there is nothing lacking in Your home. One receives when you graciously give. There is rejoicing in Your Name. Nothing is lacking in Your home.
4. The True Naam is my only support. It has satiated all my hunger. All my desires are fulfilled. O Saintly ones, profess love for His Word. The True Naam is my only support.
5. The 5-celestial tones vibrate in my being, the 'word' infused with His spirit resides within. The five demons of desire within are subdued and 'time' is overcome. Those fortunate ones who attain such pre-ordained destiny are attached to the Divine. O Nanak, they are at peace and the sound current vibrates in their homes.
6. (40th stanza) I hear the unstruck melody of pure bliss. It resounds in that fortunate abode where Your Naam resonates. You help me to slay the five demons. They whose destiny you have pre-ordained, are attached to Your Naam. Such fortunate ones obtain peace and, in their homes, plays the celestial strain.

(It is important to note that scriptural verses are shrouded in esoteric turns of phrase. Some phrases are readily understood, others require deep contemplation/introspection.)

3

THE 'SIKHIYA', THE 'LAVAN' AND THE SIKH 'GOD'

An ideal **Anand Karaj** should be a serene mix of the importance of its spiritual import and perhaps practical advice for a long and successful marital life. It should be a fulfilling, celebratory yet spiritually moving and memorable ceremony for all attending, and mainly for the couple.

This part will deal with the 'spiritual' aspect and the last part will be about more mundane matters. After all marriages might be made in heaven but must be lived out on earth!

The Anand Karaj is conducted before **Guru Ji**. (Sri Guru Granth Sahib is our Guru, the True Teacher, symbolically God Almighty) and witnessed by the **sangat** - the holy congregation the feminine counterpart of Waheguru.

The Sikh God

To understand the relationship of a Sikh couple (husband and wife) with God, it is important to attempt to grapple with the concept of the Sikh 'God'.

The Sikh 'God', though gender neutral as **'It'** is an energy source which is the 'source of all reality' and beyond the limitations of the human intellect, differs from agnosticism because though beyond the comprehension of human intellect, Sikhs develop a very loving, intimate relationship with this 'source of all existence'. In English, due to language limitations, Sikhs do refer to God in the male gender – He, Him and His. Besides countless other descriptions and attributes by which 'He' is addressed Sikhs look upon God as the Father, Mother, Brother, Friend and such intimate relationships - even Husband *(Peti-Permayshar)*. Yet Sikhism defers from the Abrahamic concept of God, Allah, Jehovah which has a tendency of 'humanising' Him – that He can be loving and yet angry, destructive and so on. Sikhism does subscribe to the basic Indic belief of re-incarnation and the Law of Karma operating under His **Hukm** (Divine Law). This does help explain to us that God is not to be blamed for disasters and calamities which are our own doing, under the umbrella of His Divine **Will** Hukm, and the Law of Karma, and finally His Grace.

Jeha beejai so lunai. Karma sendeda khet. (SGGSp133) What you sow, so shall you reap. Such is karma - the field of cause and effect. You are your own doing and undoing. Yet a Sikh accepts unequivocally and in humility, that all good fortune comes by His Grace.

From the viewpoint of married life in Sikhism, even though the Sikh God is gender neutral, yet the Divine is also referred to as Akal Purakh – the Eternal Male signifying that all of creation is of the feminine gender.

Is Jag meh Purakh aik hai, hor segeli naar sebayi. Sabh qat bhogvai alepat rehai alakh n lekhena jayi. SGGSp591/2. In this life there is only one (eternal) Male, the rest of creation is female. He enjoys within all and yet remains aloof. He is formless and beyond human understanding, comprehension.

Hence a Sikh couple comes together for the Anand Karaj with a view to becoming husband and wife, but they are, as a couple, the feminine counterpart of Akal Purakh, on their 'godward' journey of *Grahast Marag* – the path of the Householder.

The 'Lavan'

(*Lav* literally means moving from the home of the parents to setting up one's own home.)

The spiritual essence of the Anand Karaj sets it apart from any other kind of marriage ceremony - religious or secular.

In Sikhism the couple is the feminine partner in a marriage to God, the Eternal Male - **Akal Purakh**. It signifies that the couple have stepped forth on a spiritual journey of 'one spirit in two physical bodies' on a 'God-ward' journey as bride to the Akal Purakh (Eternal Male), within this human lifetime. The spiritual aspirations and progress of the couple as a team are the glue which holds the couple together for life.

The offsprings will come, with Guru Ji's Grace and one day they will leave to fulfil their own destiny. You will give them all the love, care and proper upbringing you can. Your role is that of a caregiver and then guardian.

The wise couple also starts planning for their old age and retirement from the day they go through the ceremony. That is a synopsis of the spiritual glue that sees a married couple through life as time progresses.

Dhan pir eh n akhiyan, behen ekathay hoay. Aik jyot doay moorthi, than phir kehiyai soe. SGGSp788. (They are not said to be husband and wife, who merely sit together. They alone are considered a couple who are one 'light' in two bodies.) Husband and wife coming together as one unit (the feminine half) in a spiritual marriage to the Eternal Male - *Akal Purakh*.

The Guru (God) is the 'husband-master' *(peti-permayshar)* of the household. (*Even today there are preachers who mistakenly hold that 'peti-permaysher' means the husband is the 'God of the household' expecting the wife to worship her husband!*)

It is up to you to dabble further into the deeper significance of the four hymns (lavan), listening to which you two will encircle Guru Ji four times. There are numerous translations and interpretations available. I will merely mention the salient features, especially the meditative frame of mind you should be in, as you gently walk the four circumambulations getting closer to each other and the True Guru, with each progressive round.

The ceremony should usher in a profound spiritual shift in your outlook to life as, from an individual, you will henceforth operate as a team member with your *'jeevan sathi'*, your life partner, your spouse by your side.

Remember that you are starting this amazing spiritual journey together - as a loving couple, as one unit. You will go through many 'ups' and 'downs' in your lives, and it will be your 'spiritual bond' which will see you through thick and thin.

Hence the importance of a meditative frame of mind as you undergo this ceremony. You have both come before Guru Ji in humility for His Blessings for a long, happy, healthy, successful and fulfilling life as a couple. Your focus should be fully on Guru Ji, not on how good you look on the day, or even being conscious of those around you. Immerse yourselves in the Guru Ji.

Even though you two might think that you are the centrepiece of the ceremony, which you both are as it is your big day and where all parents, relatives and guests are concerned, the **Guru Ji** always remains the 'Chief Guest', the Master, the Lord. You both come before Him in humility for His Grace - to bless you as a couple. So, make Him the centre, the pillar of your marital life from the day of your Anand Karaj.

Hence, as you proceed through each circumambulation, below are the sublime thoughts you should be dwelling upon, in a relaxed, meditative state of mind.

Look upon the 4 circumambulations as the progression of going through the 4 stages of life:

1. **Physical**, mundane progression.
2. **Mental** stage.
3. The **spiritual** stage.
4. **Union with The Ek**, the True source of all Reality, the Divine, the 1-Force.

The spiritual aspirations and progress of the couple as a team are the glue which holds the couple together for life.

1st Lav. *Har peheldi laav parverthi karam dridaea Balram jio.* ... In the first round Guru Ji sets out the mundane responsibilities of married life. Keeping the Guru in mind, reflect on a successful materialistic life infused with spirituality as a couple. Profession, earning a living, a 'home' (a safe haven), and other material necessities, coming of children and raising them as well as you can.

The word 'dharam' (dharma) simply means LIFE's DUTY. You wish to carry out your earthly 'duties' to the best of your abilities within the pursuit of divinity.

2nd Lav. *Har doojedi lav Satgur Purakh melaya Balram jio.* ... In the second round, consider your personal temperaments and changes you might want to make mentally. You are now a 'Plus-1'. What kind of an environment do you wish for in your home for yourselves and your offsprings? What part will Guru/God play in your lives?

3rd Lav. *Har teejedi lav mun chao bheya bairagia Balram jio.* ... In the third round the mind immerses itself in its spiritual aspirations/yearnings including sewa. The focus shifts from materialistic progress to spiritual aspirations. You will find that your spiritual progress augments your material well-being. You will also realise that with time your materialistic demands recede, and you start falling back on basic necessities. The quest for the TRUTH gets stronger.

4th Lav. *Har chauthedi lav mun sehaj bheya Har paya Balram jio.* ... In the final round, I have found equipoise...I am at peace. Life's work is done. I am full of gratitude. Serene acceptance of the reality of this life - the transient nature of a time-bound existence in human form, is the ultimate sense of peace and well-being. You aspire to reach that stage one day.

It is important for an intending couple to consider as many aspects as possible of marital life - its commitments, responsibilities and pitfalls before committing oneself to the life of a householder because when the physical attraction and glitter of marriage is over then all other aspects of married life come to the fore and often lead to breakups.

Western thoughts (or popular mainstream media thoughts) about what is love, leading to marriage can seem rather whimsical when the realities of marriage come into play.

The mere existence of 'pre-nuptial agreements' these days are a clear indication of the fallibility of 'falling in love' leading to marriage. Compatibility should be of higher consideration than 'love' for each other.

In the next chapter, (Part4) we shall dabble into the ground realities of married life. After what I have witnessed of marriage as an institution in my lifetime and the alarming rate of breakups, I am now a strong believer that some form of **'marriage counselling'** should begin amongst all couples right from the beginning so that challenges of married life can be addressed right from the very start.

```
In Sikhism the coming together of two people in
holy matrimony is a union immersed in collective
                 spiritual growth.
```

4

THE 'BETISULAKHANI' – 32 FEMININE ATTRIBUTES AND MUNDANE MATTERS

It should be noted that there is no 'official' advice prescribed for a Sikh couple. But advice can be gleaned from Gurbani (the Guru, *Gurumuth*). This also allows us to keep in mind evolving times, changes in cultural attitudes, cultural differences, differing temperaments of each individual in the relationship of marriage in accordance with the shifting positions of the male and the female in modern society. So, any advice I have, though based on *Gurumuth* (Guru's Teachings), takes evolution into consideration - keeping in touch with the times.

As mentioned earlier - **Marriages might be made in heaven but must be lived on earth**. Yet, in Sikhism, the coming together of two people in holy matrimony is a union immersed in collective spiritual growth. So, in any advice on marriage in Sikhism we seek the spiritual even in the mundane. The 'spiritual' is ongoing, the mundane (maya, materialism) is temporary, illusive and time bound.

In current times fixed or arranged marriages are diminishing, so the basis of a couple coming together with a view of getting married is that elusive ingredient called 'love' ('falling in love') which can also be just infatuation or simply physical attraction.

We shall try to look beyond that because we hope for longevity of marital life. The initial attraction and even that kind of 'love' will run its course. Long lasting deep love between a couple normally comes after the marriage.

There is a tongue-in-cheek saying about modern marriages - 'Marriage is the end of a beautiful romance'. Hopefully we want to change that to **Let the Anand Karaj be the start of a beautiful lifelong romance**'. So, make this union the start of a beautiful new romance for life - which firstly means – DO NOT TAKE EACH OTHER FOR GRANTED. Work on married life on a daily basis. To be able to say, 'I love you' regularly and making small gestures to supplement that positive, vibrant environment of love and wellbeing between the two of you.

I mentioned **marriage counselling** as an integral part of marital life. This does not mean hiring a professional marriage counsellor or seeing a priest on a regular basis (thought that can be helpful too), but to be conscious and fully aware that you need to be 'working' on your married life every day. For a start any marital disagreements must not be allowed to fester. They will need to be dealt with as soon as they arise, even if it means seeking help - from parents, others you can trust or even professional help, but most importantly to always keep communication between each other open. DO NOT GO TO BED HOLDING A GRUDGE. And always remembering that the head of the house is Guru/God, not one of you. The days of the male in the relationship being the alpha are no more. Any decision about the home must be unanimous and 'Guru-based' which simply means – do not let your ego get in the way of your interaction with your partner.

With that, let us ease into some 'fun' stuff which might be of interest. For your amusement firstly try to see a Robin Williams movie - 'Licence to wed'. Very funny as you would expect generally from Robin Williams but also with some messages and lessons for a couple intending to marry.

BETISULAKHANI SACH SANTAT POOT AGEAKARI SUGAD SEROOP (SGGSp370/1) {She is blessed with 32 attributes. Truthful and unblemished is her lineage. She is obedient, wise and pleasing}.

Above is a longish gurbani shabad (hymn) - basically advice for the 'bride'. Within the hymn is the above *'pangati'* (line). Do look up this hymn and translations if you wish to understand the deeper spiritual essence of Sikh married life remembering that you, as a couple are now the feminine counterpart of the Eternal Male - *Akal Purakh* which implies that all of creation is female.

Betisulakhani, literally '32 feminine attributes', is a word/phrase which has been handed down through the ages, from Hindu/Buddhist lore and used by 5th. Sikh Master Guru Arjan Sahib Ji in this hymn. The legend refers to a king called Bikram from 100B.C. (Incidentally the north Indian lunar calendar is also called the Bikrami calendar.) He was reputed to have 32 consorts and each of them had a specific virtue which was deemed essential towards a successful marriage!

Sikhism suggests that the couple is the feminine counterpart of the Eternal Male, God - Akal Purakh. **So, these feminine traits must exist in the couple, not just the bride**. The western maxim – 'get in touch with your feminine side' takes on a greater significance in Sikh philosophy.

I have come across 2 separate lists of these virtues and all are based mainly on traditional roles of the female. Today the roles are intertwined within the couple. In this age where the traditions are evolving, there is equality between husband and wife not only in words but in deeds too. **I believe that 'you' the couple should come up with your own *betisulakhani*.** It is a way for you to be proactive in your marriage. I can only give you pointers based on what I have gathered, from the old texts and changing times within my lifetime. The traditional roles of the husband being the breadwinner and the wife being a housewife raising the children, managing the home etc does not generally apply anymore.

I look upon Sikhism more as a tool for self-improvement than a 'religion'. So, my suggested *betisulakhani* are generally based on Sikh thought, Sikh spirituality.

1. HEAD OF THE HOME: Always remember that the Head of the Home is Guru/God. Some Sikhs have a painting of Guru Nanak with the heading - **Baba Nanak is the Head of this Home**... to remind themselves that all decisions must be made with Guru Ji in mind.
2. TRUTH: The first ideal in Sikhism is Truth. To seek the Truth and lead a truthful life. *Secho orai sabhko, upar sach achar* (SGGSp62). {Truth is the highest virtue, higher still is truthful living.} This also means transparency between husband and wife. We shall add trust and respect for each other.

3. CHARDHI KALA: Always look at the bright side. In disagreement look for positives. In a sad or negative situation look for the silver lining. There is always a way of turning any disagreement into a positive even if it sometimes means giving way. Insist on an upbeat disposition. Spread an aura of positivity and cheerfulness around you.

4. SPOUSE FIRST: Your life-partner always comes first. Marriages do not last if the marriage partner is not treated as No.1 in your life.

5. TWO SETS OF PARENTS: You now have two sets of parents. Treat them on an equal footing.

6. TWO FAMILIES: You now have two families around you - your family (brothers and sisters) and your spouse's family. This is also your support base in life.

7. HUKM: You live under the Law, the universal law, God's Will - HUKM. A cardinal principle for a Sikh. Life and death are in God's Will, and we accept all calamities without question. This stoic temperament binds a couple to acceptance of Guru/God being the head of the household and the base of one's spiritual journey forward.

8. TEMPERAMENT: YOU **ARE NOW A PLUS ONE (+1)**. Are there changes which you need to make to your own temperament, to be more accepting of the role you now play as a spouse and homemaker? For example, being accepting of advice, but not overly influenced by others - friends, relatives, even parents? You are stepping into a brand-new phase of life. You are no more alone. You have a soul mate and will need to be transparent, intimate and 'share' your life forward with this person.

9. LUST: Keeping in control one's lust, not only sexual, but lust for power, wealth and fame (the 3 cardinals of *maya*, materialism).

10. ANGER: Never 'lose' your temper. Anger can be a powerful servant when the need arises, but a bad master. It leads to family violence and destroys relationships.

11. GREED: Greed can consume one's life and destroy lives around you.

12. ATTACHMENT: Always keep in mind the 'reality' of this time-bound human existence. Over-attachment to anything of a materialistic nature only leads to pain and anguish. Sikhism advocates an inner detachment and outer attachment. Love like there is no tomorrow, with a passion remembering that it is all time-

bound. As mentioned earlier dharam (dharma) simply means carrying out one's earthly duty in this time-bound existence.

13. EGO: A potent negative force which destroys relationships if not shackled. Replace the 'I' with 'we' when dealing with household matters and between the couple.

14. SLANDER & GOSSIP: Both generate negative energy. They are averse to your personal well-being.

15. BUDGET: A tight and conscious control of the household budget not only ensures astute financial planning but also leads to marital harmony. *Two main monetary problems which I have observed leading to breakups are – high maintenance where the wife is concerned (hairdressing, pedicures, manicures, and clothes) and for the men, gambling, alcohol, late nights, partying and even video games.*

16. CHARITY: Within that budget must be an element of charity. Spiritually this acts as a blessing on one's finances. We call it *daswandh* - ensuring that at least 10% of your income is for charity of your choosing. Charity also brings happiness and well-being, gratitude that one is in a position to help others. This is part of your *sewa* (self-less service.)

17. FRAUD: Alertness on conmen, fraudulent dealings, scams, business or enterprise deals which are too good to be true etc. To be astute, and vigilant with one's household finances. No 'get rich quick' schemes. Even success in such schemes leads to marriage breakups!

18. CHILDREN: NO differentiation or any negative thoughts on gender or any affliction. EVERY child is precious and should be brought up with the same love and affection. This is a divine duty of a parent. *(Female infanticide is common amongst Indians even today, boys allowed to do as they please, but the girls not allowed to do the same as their brothers, and now we also see the adverse treatment of children who have problems with their gender.)*

19. GUARDIANS TO CHILDREN: As parents remember you are guardians entrusted to bring up each child as well as you can. They do not BELONG to you. One day they must find their own way.

20. CHILDREN's SPIRITUAL EDUCATION is your responsibility. School education is for their future vocation. Spiritual direction, respect for others especially elders

and general social etiquette, being hospitable, and moral behaviour is your responsibility.

21. RETIREMENT PLANNING: Do not depend on your offsprings for your retirement. Plan for your retirement right from the outset. (The days when it was naturally assumed that the male offsprings will take care of parents in their old age is fast diminishing.) This means not doing everything for your children. What are your future plans and aspirations together?

22. QUALITY TIME: With spouse and very importantly with children. It leads to healthy happy relationship. It is an important part of the education and balanced growing up of offspring.

23. HOUSEHOLD CHORES: EVERY family member must be able and involved in household chores starting with husband and wife and then every child from a very young age. Teach children responsibility.

24. HOME: Decor, atmosphere, environment. Does it create a 'safe place' for all house members and an environment of well-being? Is each house member catered for?

25. FRIENDS/RELATIVES: Are all friends/relatives conducive to a harmonious environment when they visit? Learn to cull toxic friends and relatives early.

26. PLAYING HOSTS: Are you creating a home which is hospitable? Are offsprings being taught how to be hospitable?

27. PARENTING: Children are by nature smart enough to play one parent off against the other if they sense and are exposed to differences in parenting approach of each. Mum and dad must work as a team.

28. Expecting to change certain habits of spouse in long run. How often have I heard – 'I thought he will change after marriage!'

29.

30.

31.

32. DAILY BATTLE WTH SELF: *'Khalsa so jo nth keray jung'*. A Khalsa is one who is ever at war with oneself… to be a better person each day – a better spouse, better parent, better human being.

To date I have reached this number, with input from couples I have seen through their Anand Karaj over the decades. YOU WILL FIND OTHER FACTORS WORTH ADDING TO THIS LIST TO REACH 32. That is part of your marriage counselling!

Be your own marriage counsellor. **Encourage each other further with the attributes you see in each other and help each other with the shortcomings you see in each other in an environment of love, transparency and non-judgement.** For example, one parent has a tendency of snapping at the children when they err which kids always do. The other should discuss, away from earshot of the child, such behaviour which is not healthy for the child's progress and disturbing the harmony within the home. You are now a team. You will work together.

What does your future family look like?

Some Reasons for Breakups

The main reasons I have seen marriages break down are:

1. Not prepared to change the old self-centred lifestyle expecting the partner to tag along or be there as a convenience.
2. Financial disagreements.
3. Over-interference from parents, relatives, societal pressures.
4. Infidelity
5. The wife is 'high maintenance' (numerous visits in a month to the hairdresser, manicures, pedicures, make-up) or the husband still behaves like a carefree bachelor with late nights, (bars, pubs, nightclubs) and alcohol and even addiction to TV and video games!
6. The ease at which marriages can be dissolved these days.

Every effort needs to be made to 'till death us do part'. Remember, children need a two-parent family for a balanced upbringing, notwithstanding what media, sitcoms, movies, social media etc advocate these days where the single parent is slowly becoming the norm. Even western governments encourage this by paying single parent subsidies. There will, however, be circumstances where a single parent situation exists mainly when toxicity enters a marriage relationship. A strong stable single parent is better than toxic parents under the same roof, and sometimes two separated parents perhaps work better than being together for the sake of the children.

Marriages that Work

Some observations on successful marriages:

1. Husband and wife complement each other, and their roles blend comfortably without one partner resenting his/her contribution.
2. Husbands showing care and assisting wives in roles which are traditionally considered to be the wife's role, like the upbringing and care of the offsprings and helping around the house. Sharing the household chores.

3. Husband happy to allow the wife to 'wear the pants' so to speak simply because the wife is more efficient at it (especially household expenses) but being there to assist wherever needed.
4. Neither husband nor wife are overly influenced by parents who are overbearing – hence always being by the side of the spouse.
5. Finances are well managed by both or one spouse. Full transparency in all dealings. Do not just assume responsibility but also do not just shirk responsibility and delegate it. Talk about it.
6. By mutual agreement, one partner is prepared to help the other in his or her vocation or business and to play a supportive role.

In life one has five basic needs: mental, physical, emotional, financial and spiritual. Once upon a time your partner was supposed to fulfill all five aspects of life. Having that much responsibility and dependency on one person seems a lot to handle. Seeking support elsewhere can be important and necessary. Some people are more spiritually inclined. Some more mentally stimulated. As a couple it is important to talk about all five areas and know where your support will come and what the expectations on each other are. For example, there was no point asking me what colour to paint the walls. Not because I do not care, but because I am happy with anything. It is not important that I need to be part of that decision making process. But my wife needs guidance, assurance, a second opinion. My "whatever you like" is not supporting her needs. Communication and understanding is crucial.

CONCLUSION

The *Janam Sanskar* or *Naamkaran* (Child Naming and Initiation into Sikh faith ceremony) is the spiritual spark bringing a newborn into the Sikh way of life. The *Amrit Sanchar* (ceremony to join the fraternity of the Khalsa) is the ignition not only into *Khalsahood* but more importantly to become a *gurmukh* - one who listens and follows the teachings of the Guru. The *Anand Karaj* is the spiritual kickstart to a lifelong, happy and fulfilling life of a householder the Sikh way – one soul in two physical bodies in union with the source of all reality – Waheguru.

Two Sikhcentric words augur well for success in life and especially in married life. *Chardhikala* is an ever-present upbeat, optimistic state. It is a frame of mind when one understands that whatever the circumstances one remains optimistic - looking for the silver lining, avoiding arguments and always looking for solutions to avoid negativity, never defeated. This state is the launchpad to success. *Anand* is a state of equipoise – balance in life accepting the good and the bad with the same serene stoic frame of mind. *Chardhikala* is an ever-present and necessary state of mind to understand and accept *Anand*.

The purpose of this short 'course' is firstly to arm the couple with the information and basic knowledge of *Grahasth Marg*, the path of a householder, the Sikh way. This course is not an end word, it is merely a start in the right direction. The reading of this book and going through the experience of the *Anand Karaj*, is meant to raise further curiosity and questions. That leads to further self-research, reflection and introspection towards the attainment of intuitive and experiential knowledge which leads to wisdom and emancipation. The materialistic journey within a spiritual journey as a couple begins…

HEARTIEST CONGRATULATIONS ON YOUR PREPARATIONS FOR YOUR ANAND KARAJ.
GURU DHI MEHER AND CHARDHI KALA.

SUNDRY
(Some further reflections)

There is in existence a current edict from *Akaal Takhat* that all *Anand Karaj* must take place in a gurdwara. It is at best vague because at one time there was an understanding that if there was no *gurdwara* available close by, then the ceremony could be held elsewhere. A fresh edict claims that 'destination' *Anand Karaj* based Sikh weddings are forbidden. There is also an edict that Guru Ji cannot be transported from one location to another unless *'5 Pyaray'* are present.

I do not spell out exact wordings and facts about such edicts because over the last few decades, I have seen random edicts like these come and go or become dormant. So much so that they seem rather meaningless and knee-jerk reactions bowing to the lobby of pressure groups rather than meaningful edicts which are well thought out, meaningful and carried out after some consensus.

At the point of writing, the SGPC (which virtually controls *Akaal Takhat*) and the management of the *Akaal Takhat* stand in disrepute as these Sikh central organisations have been allowed to be politically manipulated. My mention of all the above is because of what I am about to write specifically pertaining to *Anand Karaj*, the transportation of Guru Ji and the ban on 'destination' weddings.

Anand Karaj in Punjab

We will begin with my personal observations of the general Anand Karaj in Punjab. Though I am born and have lived all my life outside Punjab and India, I have attended numerous *Anand Karaj* in Punjab. Frankly I was shocked! An *Anand Karaj* of a niece specifically comes to mind.

Generally, in Punjab a Sikh 'wedding' is inevitably held in a 'marriage palace'. These are all over the state (great business!) as a convenient means of receiving the bridegroom's party, - the *baraat or junj* (*milni* ceremony), guests, reception, photography, entertainment etc. Every requirement of a traditional and cultural nature is conveniently carried out with space and playground equipment for the kids to have a good time. Very importantly loads of food from different parts of the world and drinks (alcoholic too) flowing freely.

So, in accordance with the edict that the Anand Karaj must take place in a gurdwara, the nearest village gurdwara to the marriage palace is booked at a particular time (normally for half an hour) for the Anand Karaj.

On the Mullanpur Road, for example, between Ludhiana and Mullanpur, in the Malwa region, a distance about 20km. there are over one hundred such marriage palaces, all doing a roaring trade every Friday, Saturday and Sunday. The gurdwaras in the vicinity who do very well financially can cater for up to 8 Anand Karaj per weekend days including Fridays. At half an hour of time needed per ceremony, a gurdwara can have the first Anand Karaj at say 9.30am and stretch to the mid-afternoon.

I shall describe one such 'wedding'.

Food Stall holders, the bar employees, the live band, disc jockey, sound equipment and other paraphernalia not provided by the marriage palace, arrive from dawn to be set up. (The marriage palace is already permanently decorated with plastic flowers, buntings etc.)

Depending on the booking for the Anand Karaj at the nearest gurdwara, the bride's party minus the bride normally arrives by 9.30am and ready themselves at the entrance for the *baraat* armed with garlands and gifts including gold rings for the groom's father and selected male relatives. (At the wedding I am describing there were over 20 gold rings to be gifted – to the (male) members of the baraat!) A Granthi Sahib waits in readiness to do the Ardaas. The *baraat* arrives at about 10am with a brass band. The groom arrives on a white mare or even a gaudily decorated elephant. The '*milni*' takes place after the Granthi Sahib offers a standing litany, the *ardaas*. Much hugging and lifting of opposite-side relatives takes place and the gifts are handed over. The groom is led to his designated chair with an empty chair beside him for his bride. She arrives and is seated beside him. Meanwhile the bar is opened and soon after that, the food stalls. The celebrations begin.

About 20 close relatives from both parties with the couple excuse themselves from the festivities to head to the gurdwara for the Anand Karaj at the booked time. And at the gurdwara as one wedding party arrives, one is already completing its 'lavan' and leaving. The *lavan* are completed within about 20 minutes and the party rushes back to the marriage palace to join in the merriment and the couple take their chairs for the photography session which can take over two hours while the live band and disc-jockey strut their stuff as loudly as they can while some guests get up to dance and others drink and eat and try to shout above the music to be heard! Each and every guest lines up to stand behind the couple to have their photograph taken normally as families. The children enjoy themselves on the playground with plenty of food and drinks.

By about 5pm. Some highly intoxicated guests stagger off or are carried off to their vehicles (some men without their turbans) to be taken home or the hotels.

The bride meanwhile heads off first to her parents' house to ready herself to depart and the groom follows shortly to take her back with the baraat. They take their leave to much crying from the family of the bride.

All this supposedly falls within the various edicts from Akaal Takhat and our custodians of the faith (*dharam dhe thekedar*).

Destination Weddings

I have had the privilege of conducting many destination *Anand Karaj* over the last 3 decades – various locations in USA, Canada and UK; Phuket, Krabi and Hua Hin in Thailand; Istanbul in Türkiye and Bali in Indonesia.

I specify my conditions ensuring that the sanctity of the Anand Karaj is maintained in a location which is alcohol and meat free; proper housing of the Guru Sahib for the duration of

Guru Ji being there; *degh* to be prepared in a kitchen which is well cleaned out. It is also my condition that Guru Ji is the last guest-of-honour to arrive, even after the arrival of the couple, and the first to depart immediately after the ceremony. Guru Ji is treated with full respect at all times and a dedicated *amritdhari* sewadhar is designated to serve Guru Ji around the clock.

Like many other edicts from Akaal Takhat including those pertaining to Anand Karaj in my lifetime have been kneejerk reactions and passed to satisfy certain elements who like to portray themselves as custodians of the faith and when all else fails they become bullies to enforce their will.

Anand Karaj is a sacred moving ceremony as important, in my view, to the *Amrit Sanchar* and needs to be carried out with proper understanding of its deep sacred import for the well-being of the couple into their future. To treat it as a mere ritual destroys that mystical purpose and it becomes another noisy, colourful form of entertainment for those attending – nothing more.

The destination Sikh weddings which I have conducted, with proper planning of the sacred Anand Karaj and with proper loving respect for Sri Guru Granth Sahib, have proven very beneficial to the couples involved, in their ongoing life in *Grahasth Marag*.

If a couple feels strongly enough and can afford it, then I see no reason why they cannot have their Anand Karaj wherever they wish. It makes the ceremony memorable for them and, if all conditions of maintaining the sanctity and respect of Guru Ji can be met, I see no reason why they cannot do that. Respect for Guru Ji is a personal matter. It cannot be dictated by others.

I would like to thank all my
3 daughters

Jamel, Harsel and Parvyn

firstly, for always being there to assist me
in conducting the ceremony wherever I
am needed,
and for their invaluable input into this
book.

ABOUT THE AUTHOR – DYA SINGH

Dya Singh is a world-renowned spiritual musician, writer, and community elder whose life's work has revolved around service, song, and soulful dialogue. Born and raised in Malaysia with ancestral roots in Punjab, and proudly calling Australia home for over four decades, Dya Singh has carved out a unique path blending Sikh spirituality with intercultural understanding and modern-day relevance.

A pioneer in the global Sikh music movement, Dya Singh has taken kirtan beyond traditional borders — fusing sacred sounds with world music influences and sharing messages of peace, love, and humanity with audiences across five continents. His recordings are widely available on all major streaming platforms and YouTube, continuing to inspire listeners across cultures and generations.

Beyond the music, Dya Singh is deeply committed to empowering the next generation of **Young Sikh professionals**, and reshaping the **image of Sikhs in the wider community** through education, interfaith dialogue, and cultural storytelling. He is a respected voice in Australia's interfaith landscape and a regular columnist for *Star News* alongside his eldest daughter, Dr Jamel Kaur Singh.

Dya Singh's greatest source of pride, however, lies in his family. With gratitude to his beloved daughters — **Jamel**, **Harsel**, and **Parvyn** — and his cherished grandchildren — **Saahiel**, **Saffal**, **Khiaan**, and **Ravi** — he continues his journey of reflection and service with heart and humility.

"Service is the rent we pay for our time on this planet." Dya Singh.

Previous books available on Amazon:
Sikhing Success and Happiness
The Zen of Sikhing

In the pipeline is, *Sikhing the Avatar Within*, *The Accidental Raggi* (a Semi Autobiography) and who knows what will come next!